Watersafe Your Baby in One Week

Watersafe Your Baby in One Week

by
Danuta Rylko

Foreword by
Bradford Luz, Ph.D.

▲
▼▼
Addison-Wesley Publishing Company
Reading, Massachusetts • Menlo Park, California
London • Amsterdam • Don Mills, Ontario • Sydney

797. 21
RyLko

Library of Congress Cataloging in Publication Data

Rylko, Danuta.
    Watersafe your baby in one week.

    1. Swimming for infants--Study and teaching.
I.   Title.
GV837.25.R94   1983   797.2'1'0880542   83-2707
ISBN 0-201-10898-4

The instructions in this book represent a program developed by the author over many years. If adhered to faithfully, this program can teach a child the skills she needs to survive water accidents. The publisher accepts no responsibility for accidents occurring as a result of using the techniques presented in this book.

The publisher wishes to thank the American Red Cross and the American Heart Association for their permission to use the safety material in Appendix B.

Originally published as *The Water Baby Book* in 1982 by Avant Books, San Diego, California.

Cover and book design: Michael Gosney and Dalia Hartman
Photo direction: Michael Gosney
Cover photo: Jim Coit
Interior photos: Bradford Luz and Jim Coit
Drawing p. 11 by Kenneth J. Wilson

ABCDEFGHIJ-HA-87543
First Printing, March 1983

Dedication

This book is dedicated to my mother, Michelle,
whose beauty and courage taught me that
all things are possible . . .

Contents

FOREWORD

When Danuta asked me to review the final draft of this book I was thrilled. I have been a water safety instructor and have owned and operated my own swim school for many years. In this time I have read just about everything printed on teaching infants and young children to swim. And working with children as I do, I am always looking for new and better resources to recommend to parents. So let me share with you what I have discovered in this book and about the "watersafe" method.

This is not just another "how-to" book. It is a step-by-step exposition of a well thought out method, refined by years of in-the-pool teaching. The author has correctly identified infant reflexes and behaviors that can be used to teach the very young to float, use breath control and to swim. The method works for the infant who has no language skills, because certain reflexes can be chained together into a swimming skill. It works for toddlers and older children, who already have the use of language and have acquired some fears, because the exercises break down so simply the mechanics and necessary skills that the child must learn.

Once a child has progressed through the series of training exercises set forth here he will be swimming. The idea behind it all is a simple one. Teach the child a skill through an exercise. Then teach another skill in such a way that it can be connected and used with both what was learned before and what will be taught next. The sum of these connected skills is the learned behavior, swimming. This is chaining bits of behavior together into one complex behavior. The end product is what the author refers to as "the six-day blitz," an accelerated method of teaching that has the child floating and swimming with some degree of control in about three hours' time. This happens because the carefully designed exercises that are a part of this method allow only one result—success.

If you, as a parent, are concerned that your child be taught with the right amount of knowhow, sensitivity and attention, then you will want your child to be taught using this method. I particularly appreciate the author's sensitivity to the needs of parents and the way this method is designed to blend the instructor, child and assistant into a learning team. Each person in the learning team has a role; all work smoothly toward the same end.

How this Method Works in Behavioral Terms

Let's take a look at how the watersafe method works in terms of learning theory. It makes no difference if we talk in terms of Hull's Behavior theory, Wolpe's Reciprocal Inhibition theory or Skinner's Operant Conditioning theory. Elements of the whole learning theory are at work in this training method. It is behavioral in nature.

For instance, Hullian theory states that certain stimuli are presented which affect the efferent nervous system of the child. This impact produces a motor response, such as a gasp or a full body extension, which can be refined into a final (desired) externalized movement. And after much repetition, the stimulus / response relationship becomes a habit so that the desired action can always occur (in this case, the behavior of breath control, turning over onto the back, and floating).

When we take this theory to poolside, we see the instructor presenting the child with a series of controlled stimulus situations through the use of cues that are part of carefully designed exercises in a six-day lesson plan. The cues trigger a close approximation to the desired response on the child's part. Here the cue is the stimulus, the child's reflex behavior is the response of the efferent nervous system and the result of this response. The final or desired behavior is the use of this response as part of the more complex behavior of swimming.

Each approximation will be rewarded and connected to other behaviors in a series. This process is known as shaping a behavior and chaining it to others to develop a complex skill. In this way what the child learns in response to carefully controlled cues in the water environment will become the child's normal response anytime he is in the water. And what is learned in one lesson will become the basis for more complex behavior of which it is a part. Thus each lesson builds on the skills learned in previous lessons.

The watersafe method pays very careful attention to the fact that swimming is a complex behavior, and thus establishes a base of skills, conditioning each contributing behavior response by response. Skills are refined over a period of time through continuous repetition until a successful approximation of the behavior desired is achieved. Correct responses are immediately reinforced. Each successful response then becomes the reinforcing event for the previous and succeeding responses.

Carefully controlled consequences are the reinforcements that strengthen the desired response and increase the later probability of its occurrence. In other words, it is important that the child be able to succeed almost every time he is placed in the learning situation, and that when he succeeds he is made aware that he has done what was desired. Hugs, verbal praise, holding and cuddling are extremely important here.

Successful Operant Conditioning requires that the exercises set out for the child have clear behavioral goals and objectives. In the development of this technique—the right exercise in the right sequence in a critical period of time—the author has been able to clearly break down and define behavioral objectives that are presented clearly to the reader. The method of presenting the cue, setting the antecedent event, and the descriptions of the response to be elicited are excellent. This allows the parent trying to reproduce this method to develop tight controls over the learning contingencies, and to carefully shape the relationship between the response and its consequence.

All of this means that the method takes the guesswork and the error out of teaching infants and young children swimming skills. Any instructor who follows this method carefully can teach and reproduce the desired behavior, be it breath control, floating, or changing the body position with any child in a water environment. The objectives of this conditioning method become the learning criteria for good performance. And the learning of the behaviors themselves becomes its own reward because they allow the child some degree of comfort and autonomy in the water.

In summary, this behavioral method establishes a basic set of physiological responses to set cues, the resulting responses being the elements of a more complex swimming behavior.

As you are probably aware, the idea of teaching a young child to swim is not all that new. In fact, the first scientific study of "swimming-like behavior" in young infants was done by Dr. Myrtle McGraw in 1939. The infants she studied ranged in age from eleven days to two and one-half years. She observed the following ranges of reflex, skills and ability.

She found that newborn infants, up to five months, exhibit breath control and swimming reflexes when submerged in water. After six months, and with the evolution of the switchover to voluntary motor control, certain reflexes disappear, and infants then have to learn to organize and coordinate movements like those involved in swimming. From eight months on the child becomes more practiced at voluntary control of its movements and has the ability to make smoother and fuller motions. Learning becomes easier. By eighteen months of age the child has begun to master language and can use this as a learning tool as well.

We can see that the skills taught and developed by this technique are well within the range of infant and young child abilities. Swimming and water play can be fun, develop coordination and strength, and build the child's sense of self-mastery.

In this technique infant reflexes that appear at birth and later evolve into more complex and voluntary behavior become the raw materials which the instructor observes and works with to teach lasting water survival skills. Reflexes, which are the natural behaviors and responses of the infant, are woven into a fabric of behavioral cues, immediate rewards and close physical support. From this material the child is able to cut a set of water skills he can use all of his swimming life.

Based on McGraw's work we see that young infants float better than they can swim. And, as Danuta shows, they can learn to hold their breath, roll over to float on their backs, and float indefinitely. The infant who learns this behavior can save his own life, and can enter into water play with his parents. Having had the chance to see this method in action I can say that the results produced were simply brilliant, and most effective.

Part of the controversy that surrounds the teaching of young infants to swim is that between six and eighteen months they seem to forget or lose some of their swimming skills. As we have noted earlier, during this period of the child's development reflexes are developing into more complex neuromuscular patterns that are voluntary. The method presented here deals with this problem well. What has been learned by the child is stored in his motor memory. When the parent and the instructor take the child into the water during this period of development, they use behavioral cues to teach and to jog the child's motor memory. This helps to eliminate confusion for the child and allows him to succeed in developing and using swimming skills.

What the child seems to forget can be brought back for his use in a matter of minutes with the use of the now familiar exercises. This skill then becomes the platform from which other water games and more coordinated swimming strokes can be learned.

There have been many books written on the topic of teaching young children to swim and a few on teaching infants since Dr. McGraw's study. But this book stands out as the best training manual for both age groups to date. It is a superior teaching tool, written clearly in cheerful and playful style. The illustrations and photos allow the exercises described to be reproduced by the instructor with exactness. This book gives the reader the feeling of its being well crafted as a teaching aid.

Watersafe Your Baby in One Week is neither a summary nor a repetition of other methods. It is an independently conceived and unique approach to the teaching of infants and young children. The method discussed develops the reflex behaviors of infancy into a set of coordinated and lasting survival skills. These skills can then be used as the basis from which to develop more complex and demanding swimming skills as the child's development permits. The infant is taught that water is a natural and easily mastered environment, full of enjoyable experiences. With the mastery of these skills they become the child's natural response when in the water.

The author's style with children really comes through in each chapter. Here is evidence of a woman who is extremely knowledgeable about young children. There is also love, concern and a rare playfulness that are an integral part of each exercise. They are a part of the method, too. This technique seems to blend the right amount of challenge and demand for performance with a respect for the child's individual limits and learning style. Useful examples of clear and effective communication between adult and child abound in this book.

I feel that this method can make the learning of water skills a shorter, more positive, and more successful learning experience for both the child and the parent. I am pleased to recommend this book and this method to parents and swim instructors everywhere. Any healthy infant or young child can learn these life-saving skills quickly, and so can any swim instructor.

Brad Luz, Ph.D.

INTRODUCTION

Babies and Water—A Natural Combination!

Tiny humans are capable, thinking, intelligent, sensitive, coordinated, strong, courageous, tough, and sturdy little critters. They are growing sponges of information. They are "on the job" every waking hour learning to live. A baby's prime function is to learn—to learn about Mommy and Daddy, colors, sounds, textures, schedules, puppies, peas and carrots, and chocolate pudding. By twelve months old, many babies have advanced from crawling, then walking to running! So why not swimming?

Why not, indeed! Every day, the newspaper tells stories of small children losing their lives in their own backyard swimming pools. And every time I read one of these stories, my heart aches for that child and for those parents, because the tragedy and agony could have been avoided. There is no reason for a conscious child to drown. Teaching a child to save his own life in any body of water is a relatively simple procedure. Teaching a baby life-saving techniques requires about half an hour a day for six consecutive days. In less than a week, by following the daily procedures in this book, you can teach a baby water survival. You can teach an infant as young as 4 months to hold his breath, to surface after a tumble into a pool, to flip to his back, and **breathe** and **relax** and **float** . . . indefinitely—for hours if necessary—until help arrives.

I have taught **thousands** of babies this life-saving technique over the past 13 years and I have passed this method on to dozens of other instructors and hundreds of parents. I now pass this method on to you. If you have a pool nearby and a baby, I urge you to read this book and give your baby a fighting chance to survive a water accident and a headstart on enjoying the water, safely, for the rest of his life.

How It All Began

The Waterbug Swim School was born in the late 1960s at a resort near Sonoma, California. As the recreation director there I was often approached by mothers with infants, who asked if I could start a class teaching babies water survival. So many California homes came equipped with swimming pools—they were as abundant as dishwashers—that there was growing concern for the small children in these homes, who weren't prepared to cope with the water. And infant swimming programs were virtually unheard of at the time. After one desperate mother told me the tale of how her one-year-old son managed to crawl between the bars of their brand-new $1,000 pool fence, and then fell in before she could catch up with him, I decided to start a class for babies. Little did I know then that

babies are just as capable of surviving alone in the water as bigger people! As a matter of fact, in those early days the babies taught ME what they were capable of doing. I merely supplied them with the opportunity to learn.

Those little ones taught me well. For example, I learned quickly that if there were more than one or two babies in the water at the same time, they tended to share their emotions: if one cried, they all cried. That's when I learned a one-to-one approach was more comfortable for everyone concerned. Also, it was easy enough to teach a baby to hold his breath and swim under water — that can be accomplished in just minutes. What takes more time is teaching the little thing to stay above the water. After all, that's what survival is all about!

That summer over one hundred babies graduated from my water skills class. The following year I was flooded with requests to continue the infant swim program, and the Waterbug Swim School for Infants was founded. The beauty of the school was its privacy. The classes were all taught in home pools. Apart from the luxury Mom had of not having to tote the tot and bags of clothes and cookies across town, the baby was comfortable with the familiarity of home — and it made practicing really convenient as well. The method was streamlined, during those years, into the present six-day course, allowing flexibility for children of various ages, from infants to toddlers.

Through the years Waterbugs grew from two instructors to over 20 and expanded to San Francisco, Phoenix, and later to San Diego. With **Watersafe Your Baby in One Week**, we are making our training program available, on a broader basis, to parents and instructors.

The method is marvelous: it is unique in that it's fast, the babies remember what they learn, and it offers the best possible chance of survival for a child in water. As a bonus, the infant actually learns to swim — the crawl stroke, etc. — much earlier and easier!

A word for those who hesitate teaching their infant this survival technique: against all arguments, consider the consequences if the child is given no alternative.

This is a time of learning for you and your baby; enjoy the growth and safety together!

Danuta Rylko

Watersafe Your Baby
in One Week

SETTING THE STAGE

Please read the entire book before beginning actual training
This section contains a few teaching tips and preparatory suggestions

The Pool — Keep It Warm

The temperature of the pool should be at least 80 degrees. Babies get mighty cold mighty fast, and they won't be learning if they're too busy shivering.

Pool Chemicals — No Problem

The chlorine and soda ash that go into a pool to kill bacteria are usually not present in sufficient quantities to hurt the baby in any way.

On Bathing Suits: Put Fashion Aside For Now

Drop the drawers! Let's forget modesty for this occasion. Bathing suits, rubber pants, and diapers will only hinder the baby's movement. Baby bikinis may be cute, but they're not practical; they can be binding and uncomfortable. To make learning as easy as possible, dump the diapers! (In case there's a little "accident" in the pool, the filter will do its job, and the chlorine will come to the rescue. What floats can be scooped out.)

Meeting Baby's Schedule

As every parent knows, the baby is a creature of habit, just like everybody else. Before tackling these lessons, be sure you schedule the event around the baby's clock, not yours! The baby should not be fed for at least one or two hours before the lesson—and make that a light meal! Fit the lessons around his nap time. Nothing is worse than a grouchy baby!

Sunburn!

Baby skin is fine and tender; protect it! Put some sunblock on his cheeks and shoulders. But you may end up with a slippery little "son-of-a-gun" if you douse the baby completely with oil. So use it sparingly. A light T-shirt protects skin as well and makes the baby easier to hold.

No Help Wanted — Quiet Zone

Post these signs at poolside. No curious neighbors, worried relatives, frisky puppies, barking dogs or banjo players allowed. The last thing you need is a lot of distraction. You want to get the message across to your new swimmers that water is a peaceful, gentle environment. One of the reasons why group swim classes for infants are so often unsuccessful is that the noise in such an environment creates anxieties. That really puts a damper on the one-to-one relationship you are trying to set up. So keep the lesson quiet — between you and the baby and the water — with no distractions. One way to ensure the success of the lessons is to hold them in a **private** pool.

The Baby's Ready, But Are You?

If your hands sweat at the thought of tackling the next six days of swimming lessons, then for Pete's sake don't do it! If you're at all anxious or nervous about your capacity as an instructor, the baby will know it! Don't feed each other's fears. If you like the water, so will your baby. If you don't, find someone else who does.

Eye Contact

Try not to look like the Monster From The Blue Lagoon. No big sunhats or garish sunglasses. Baby will want to identify you as another human being. Eye contact is reassuring. If the baby can't see your eyes, he can't see **you**!

Voice Contact

Your voice is going to be your baby's source of confidence and security. Soothing tones are infectious. **At all times**, keep your voice **low and calm, no matter what**. It's not what you say, but how you say it. Be there visually and verbally with your baby. Your voice and your face are proof of your reassuring existence.

The Art of Holding

Babies need security. So when you hold that baby, really hold him! Make every hand-hold count! If the baby's arms or feet are dangling, he will not feel secure. Children are not meant to be handled like spaghetti or overripe fruit, **so take hold!**

Kicking: Not Now!

For the same reason the baby sometimes overarches when first learning this back business, some babies start **kicking** to relieve their nerves. Usually this isn't much of a problem because babies will kick only so hard while at the same time maintaining a beautiful float. But others kick so hard and fast that they splash water in their faces, which gets them even more anxious. So they kick harder, more water gets in their eyes and, well, you get a snowballing waterbug who'd be better off playing soccer!

Waiting it out is just about the only way to solve this problem. But this could take some time! Babies don't usually get tired too fast from kicking and some have been able to keep it up all lesson long. The best thing to do is to make sure the baby is completely relaxed. With the child quiet and comfortable, the kicking will eventually stop. (There are cases where some babies will kick their little feet off in perfect back float control, propelling themselves like mini-motorboats all around the pool!)

DAY
1

Getting Acquainted

Standing in the shallow end of the pool with the baby in one arm, wet him down with the other. Wet his arms, legs, back and tummy, face and hair. **No dunking shock treatments!**

Keeping the baby at arm's distance from you, hold him (firmly) under his arms and get him used to being away from your body. We want more water around the baby, and the least amount of physical contact with the instructor possible, except when it's time for hugs and kisses.

Start walking around the pool, gently swishing the baby through the water. Slowly get the water level up to the baby's chest and then his shoulders while you're walking, talking and distracting him from what you're doing. Let the water find its way to his chin. Still walking around the pool, tilt the baby a little and get one cheek wet, then the other.

Repeat this tilt, but this time get half the baby's face wet, including his ear. We are gradually getting the baby's head totally immersed in the water, but by **tilting** the baby, and **continuously moving through** the water. This way the water is always directed **away** from the baby's face. We are not jamming water up baby's nose; the water tends to trickle across his face gently rather than gushing around him from all directions.

Going Under

Once the baby has adjusted to water near his face, he is ready to go **under** the water. This isn't as awesome as it sounds. Begin by giving the baby a little uplift as a cue that something is about to happen. Then smoothly and quickly swish him sideways through the water, lower and lower, until he's under the water. He should be under water 3 to 4 seconds. Bring him up and out just as smoothly as he went in, and keep talking as if nothing happened. Nine times out of ten, the baby won't know what happened, but he **will** hold his breath!

If he's not sputtering, you know that he's done it right. Wait a few moments and bring the baby under the water again and again, until you feel he's used to it. Chances are the baby won't be fussing because you've gone slow enough with him. If he cries, that's okay — calm him down a bit and do it again. Now, before we go on, there are some things you need to know.

Swishing, swishing . . . under!

Cueing

An example of a cue was that little uplift and jerk you gave the baby before he went under the water each time. Cues are vital; they "tell" the baby when he's going under the water so he can prepare himself for it. (That little jerk will cause the child to momentarily gasp and hold his breath.) After the first

one or two times, he understands what that cue means. Cues eliminate surprises and let the baby in on what's happening. **Use them each time the baby goes under the water.**

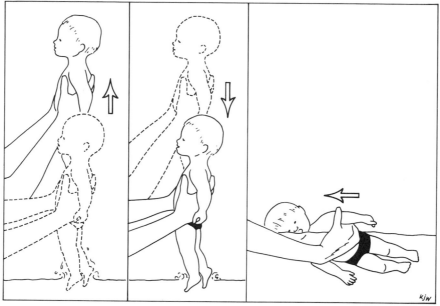
The cue.

Going Under Pointers

It's not necessary for the baby to close his mouth to hold his breath, so don't worry if his hatch is open.

- **Never** give a false cue. If you cue, follow through whether or not you think the baby was ready. If he can rely on your consistency, he will adjust to your timing.
- **Always** move the baby sideways through the water, keeping the wet stuff moving past the baby's face. Never dunk!
- Always be smooth. Uncertainty on your part or tenseness of any kind will make the baby feel insecure.
- **Always watch the baby's face.** If the baby is holding his breath, you will see **a silver bubble of air** in each nostril when he's under water. If you don't see the bubbles listen to the baby's breathing when he comes up. If he's breathing clearly — no sputtering or coughing — there's no problem. If the baby does choke, work on your cue — he's not getting the message. The sputtering shouldn't last long, and the baby will control his breath within a very short period of time because

he will learn to read your cues. Be patient and keep trying!

~ If the baby is tense or disturbed, step back a few paces, and go back to swishing waist-deep, then chest-deep, and work back up to the underwater exercises.

Signs of Distress

It's easy to tell when the baby has had enough water for the day. Shivering due to loss of body heat or a pale blue coloring about the mouth due to constriction of the blood vessels are clear signs that physical limits have been reached. But don't wait that long. Get the child out of the pool; wrap him in a big, fluffy towel to restore body heat. A vigorous hand rub over the towel will get the warm blood circulating again.

If He Doesn't Hold His Breath...

Don't worry! The baby has to **learn** to hold his breath — that's what the lessons are all about! If the baby is to learn what's right, he has to know what's wrong. If he isn't holding his breath, he's probably drinking the water, not inhaling it. This means it's going to his stomach, not his lungs. Pat him on the back, give him a hug, and try the exercise again. When given the chance to clear his breathing with a little rest, soon the water is coughed up — much like drinking a glass of water and having it go down the "wrong way."

A Word On Burps

After drinking some pool water, his tummy is going to get full, just as if he's had a full meal. He's going to have to burp — the same way he burped when he had a full bottle of milk. And, just like a burp, there will be some spew on your shoulder or wherever. This is not vomiting. Every parent knows the difference between burping and throwing up!

Burping is as much the result of swallowing air as it is of swallowing water. When babies first learn to hold their breath, they don't know what to do with it. They have little chipmunk cheeks full of air, and what now? They swallow it, that's what. After a few gulps of air the tot's tummy becomes light as a balloon. If the baby gets cranky, it's possible that it's burping time. Put the baby on your shoulder, tap him on the back, and wait for the burp. Sometimes it's forceful — it could put a beer drinker to shame!

If the burp is difficult to get up, it could be that the baby is cold, and cold tummy muscles are not about to relax and let a burp through. Get down in the water and warm him up. Try pressing on the baby's tummy firmly while moving your hand around in a circular motion. If that doesn't do it, go back to swimming and try getting the burp up later. Or get out of the water and warm the baby with a towel.

A hug, a rest, and a burp.

Remember, water and air are both trapped in the baby's stomach. The force of the burp will be like bursting a balloon sometimes. The water will be forced up with the air. That's good! When his tummy is relaxed, the baby is more comfortable and we can continue with the lesson. (Now you know why it's a darn good idea not to have any food in that little tummy. It could get crowded out!)

Ending The Lesson

Ten to fifteen minutes should be more than enough time to get the baby used to being wet and to give him a taste of the underwater world. Remember, the keys to this technique are **smoothness**, **repetition** and **reinforcement**. Do the exercises often enough so that the child gets accustomed to and comfortable with them.

If the baby fusses a bit, that's okay. There is nothing wrong with crying as long as you know the reason for it. If the baby seems to be afraid, stop immediately. The "I'm afraid" cry is identified by white knuckles, terrified eyes, and one hell of a scream. If the child is not frightened but is crying for

13

other reasons, find out what they are. Does he need to burp? Is he tired? Is he cold? Are there distractions confusing and bothering him? **Never end the lesson while the baby is crying**! Little ones catch on fast and if they think they've locked onto the key to terminating the lesson by crying, they will purposely do it every time to get out of the pool. You'll have to be shrewd — one step ahead of the little swimmer. Relieve the cause of the tears and calm him down before getting out of the water. If the lesson is over for the day, then it's fine to get out. If there's more to do, then continue. But remember who's in charge of ending the lesson!

Practice

It makes things perfect. Find time later on in the day, maybe after the baby's nap, to take the baby back into the pool. Although a quick exercise here and there can't hurt, it's more important to spend about ten minutes playing. We want the baby to know that water is fun as well as work, and a "practice session" should have good amounts of undemanding playtime.

DAY ONE SUMMARY

1

Hold the baby securely.

2

Keep talking in low, reassuring tones.

3

Get wet slowly.

4

Keep the baby's body at arm's length from you.

5

Control the environment; private pool, no noise.

6

Keep the water streaming past the baby's face.

7

Cue the baby with an upward lift before bringing him under water.

8

Repeat the exercises until the baby is comfortable with them.

9

Give lots of hugs and kisses for things well done.

10

The baby sets the pace, so be in tune with his ways.

11

The end of the lesson is your decision, so don't end
on a note of tears.

12

Play with the baby in the pool later in the day and sprinkle play
with practice exercises.

DAY 2

Going Solo

Today should follow on the heels of Day One. It is terribly important that this series of lessons continue on consecutive days. The time factor right now is critical, and we don't want anything to be forgotten between now and the end of the lessons. By the last day, forgetting will be practically impossible.

If for any reason a day or two is lost during this series of lessons, you may find yourself starting at Day One all over again. Consistency is necessary in order to form habits, and if there is a break in consistency the habit will be poorly formed. Be patient if you find yourself needing to go back to Day One work at times.

Day Two primarily reinforces the breathholding exercises done in the first day's work. In addition, Day Two will give the baby a taste of being on his own under water, and a few varieties of exercises are offered to eliminate boredom.

Spend the first five minutes of today repeating everything you did with the baby on Day One. Reinforce what the baby already knows before we go on to something he doesn't know.

Solo Mio!

For his first "solo flight," cue the baby with the usual little upward jerk, and then pull him under the water **toward** you. Step back and give him a little room as you gently let go of him.

The "solo flight"—baby gliding toward you.

He will be floating face-down, underwater, his head toward you. Allow him a few seconds to feel the water around him. Then, very smoothly, as if you never let go, place your hands under the baby's arms and bring him **up** and **out** of the water. Repeat this several times until you think he is comfortable with this new sensation.

It's important for several reasons that you always stay in front of the baby when he's under water. First, you can see his face. You may be able to tell if he's swallowing water and not holding his breath. Second, the baby can see **you**, a real confidence-booster for him. And third, you're in a better position to take hold of him from the front than from his side or behind.

If the baby's breathing sounds sputtery, or wheezy, help him clear his throat, check for a burp, and then go back to the swishing and cueing exercises of Day One. He may not be holding his breath correctly. Or, you may be leaving him under the water too long, although you will find that his breath-holding capacity will increase with each day. Temper your caution. Don't hold him back, but at the same time don't push him beyond his pace. Your intuition will have to play a big part in determining his capacities.

Sitting On The Pool's Edge

Just as if you're cueing the baby and pulling him towards you under water, do the same exercise — except this time start the baby from a sitting position on the pool's edge.

With a little upward jerk (that's the cue), pull the baby gently off the side and let him fall into the water in front of you. Let him go after you have him moving towards you in an underwater glide. After a few seconds, pick him up by the armpits. Remember, no loud shouting or cheering. The suddenness of sounds and noise after the underwater calm and silence could shock him. Be calm. Sound calm.

From The Steps

This exercise is another way to vary the underwater training. Sit the baby on the steps and pull him toward you with the usual motion. Carry out the same exercise. Variety is the spice that cures boredom, so interchange these variations of the **solo flight**. Don't forget the hugs and kisses!

Breathholding Insurance

There's another way besides that of the often-elusive silver bubbles in the nostrils to insure that the baby is holding his breath. If he's under too long and loses his breath, you will be able to tell. When the baby needs air, he will first exhale the old air. When you see a big glob of bubbles rise to the surface of the water, that's it! — the exhaled old air. The baby needs to breathe; so pick him up and lift him straight out of the water. If you react quickly he won't have time to take in any water. Praise him, kiss him, and go back to the exercise again. If the baby did take in some water, give him a short rest and then try again.

Spend about 20 minutes on the lesson today, but don't overdo it! Tomorrow is a big day. Remember to **play** with the baby in the water later today.

DAY TWO SUMMARY

1

The baby goes solo today—remember to stand in front of him as he glides toward you. You see him and he sees you.

2

Check for those burps.

3

For variation, pull the baby off the steps, or off the side of the pool, and into the water toward you.

4

A large cluster of bubbles is a sign that the baby needs air. Bring him up, give him a few hugs and try the exercise again. No harm done.

5

Don't forget playtime later in the day.

DAY 3

Introducing the Back Float

Today the baby will be swimming between you and a second person whom you must arrange to have in the pool with you. Today will not only increase the baby's breathholding endurance, it will also add more exercises so that the baby will be alone under water more often. More importantly, today will give the baby his first taste of what it's like to be on his back.

Warm the baby up by repeating the exercises from Day Two. Spend five to ten minutes getting the baby wet, swishing, cueing, and going under.

Enter The Helper

Be sure your helper understands the need for smoothness, a calm voice, and cueing and holding procedures. Make sure to review the previous days' exercises. The baby is going to glide under water between the two of you.

To do this, you'll have to hold the baby differently to prepare him to swim to your aide. Place your arm under the baby's chest and hold the baby's outside arm with your hand. Tuck your other arm **under both legs** of the

Keep baby at a 45-degree angle, holding outside leg.

baby, holding the baby's outside leg with your other hand. Now the baby is lying on his tummy across both your arms and you have complete control. The baby has a sense of being securely held. With a quick upward jerk (the cue), gently place the baby at a 45-degree angle into the water, his head entering the water slightly ahead of the rest of his body. Give him a smooth shove towards your helper (whose arms are under the water, reaching out for the baby) and let go. Your helper then places his/her hands under the

baby's arms and picks him up gently, smoothly, and quietly. We stress **gently and quietly** because if the baby is anxious about this new exercise, this anxiety can be neutralized by the teacher's sense of calm. Abrupt movement and harsh, shrill, or loud sounds can be "tensifying." After a pause, give him a hug and some praise. Now it's the helper's turn to send the baby back to you.

You might appreciate knowing that in the event you or your aide makes a mistake, the baby will be forgiving. He won't get shook up if the cue isn't right the first time, or if he sputters because he didn't get enough time to catch his breath. Just because he's little doesn't mean he isn't tough. He's been in the water for three days and should be quite comfortable with it by now.

Use your judgment as to how long the baby should remain under water during this exercise. Chances are that he can hold his breath longer than you give him credit for — perhaps five or six seconds. Allow the baby to experiment with his limitations. Allow him to make mistakes. It's through your allowances and his mistakes that you both learn his limitations and skills.

Continue passing the baby between the two of you until you think he has things under control. It's not as hard as you may think and should not take more than ten minutes. **The most important part of Day Three is yet to come!**

Introducing The Back Float

Many children are not too keen about being on their backs initially, especially since it's coupled with the early insecure stages of being in the water. You will have to be particularly sneaky in getting the baby on his back without his knowing it!

Hold the baby with his back facing you. Gently encourage him to lay his head on your shoulder (see photo). Slowly bend your knees and get lower in the water. The extra water around the baby will make his body buoyant and his legs should rise to the surface. The baby is lying on you but the lower half of his body is suspended by water.

Get low enough in the water so that the baby's ears are submerged. Keep talking to him. At the first sign of discomfort, pick him up by simply standing up out of the water, extending your knee for him to sit on. Repeat this procedure, allowing the baby to adjust to this "lay back" position for longer and longer periods of time. **Important:** Keep the baby's head low, maintaining him in as close to a prone position as possible. If his head is low, his legs will be closer to the surface. The idea is to **simulate** as closely as possible the back float position, using only minimum support where and when necessary. A common error is to give the child more upper body support than he really needs. That mistake produces a feet-first sinker and we don't want that!

Simulating the back float position.

Flipping

If the baby doesn't buy your sneak approach to back floating, then go right into flipping. This takes much of the concentration of back floating away from the baby's attention and merges it with an entire set of movements — from swimming to flipping, to back floating, to sitting. The baby really has little time to dwell on the fact that "somewhere in there he was lying on his back." Sneakiness at its best!

Flipping is the procedure by which the baby **turns** from his stomach to his back — i.e., from a face-down to a face-up position in the water. Begin by pulling the baby from the steps toward you and getting him in a floating glide. Then, standing directly in front of the baby, hold his head between both your hands. Gently rotate the baby's head until his body follows through to a complete flip over to his back. The thing most instructors have trouble with here is keeping the baby's head level with the water throughout the rotation. **Don't lift the baby's head out of the water: simply turn his head from face-down to face-up.** The instant the baby is on his back, pick him up. Remember, we don't want him to **think** about being on his back yet.

As always, repeat this drill quickly, with occasional rests and hugs in between.

Turn him over by his head, keeping his body flat in the water. Once he is on his back, pick him up.

Another Way To Flip

Depending on your preferences, you might want to flip the baby onto his back by using his arm as a lever, rather than by rotating his head. As the baby approaches you in the glide, reach for one of his arms and use it to turn him from his stomach onto his back. This is handy since the baby's arms will automatically be up near his head, a position which also helps keep his legs out and up at the surface of the water. This position aids in maintaining balance. The method of rotating the baby described here will also be helpful when we get to the topic of **eliminating support** a bit later.

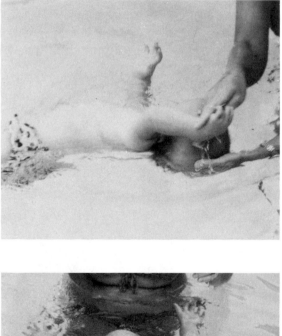

Flipping, using his arm instead of his head.

What If He Cries?

Not all babies cry during these lessons, but some may. Crying comes naturally to any baby; it's nothing to be alarmed about if you understand the reasons why. Since this is the first day he has been exposed to the back float, don't push too much. Get him used to the feeling slowly. Break up the monotony of the exercises by repeating an old exercise that he can handle more comfortably. This will renew his confidence. Then try the back float again.

Use your discretion and intuitive forces to determine the degree of the baby's anxieties. There really is a difference between a fussy, tired cry and a cry of sheer panic; between a temper tantrum and fear. Your experiences and observations with children will be called upon and tested over and over again. **Never allow the baby to reach the stage of panic!** If you sense that the anxiety level is critically high and the baby is either clinging to you, screaming, or trembling, **stop what you are doing immediately! Something is wrong!!** Babies can't talk, but they sure know how to get their message across. At this point, there could be several reasons for anxiety.

First, you may be going too fast. You may not be in tune with the baby's pace. Have you been giving him time to catch his breath? Are you hugging and reassuring him in between a succession of rapid exercises?

Second, you may not have reinforced one or more steps in the teaching progression sufficiently. If there is a weak link in the chain of progression, everything you attempt after that weak link will also be weak. For instance, if the baby has not mastered breathholding, all the underwater workouts could be frightening him.

Third, you may have caused the baby to lose his sense of self-control. If you weren't reading the messages he was giving you earlier, he could become desperate.

Whatever the problem, figure it out before you attempt to add any new material in the swimming lessons! The sooner you reduce the distress, the sooner the baby will stop **thinking about it**. Remember, at this stage of the game, the **mind** can inhibit the **body**. Keep the baby's mind occupied on something else — a toy, a bug, anything — just be sure to distract him from his troubles.

Holding the baby close has a beautiful, calming effect. Stroke his head, rock him in your arms, sit with him on the steps. Walk with him slowly around the pool. Make your arms feel strong and secure around him. Be extremely quiet. Try a little simple swishing; renew his confidence with an extra-simple exercise and build from there. **By no means leave the water while the baby is unhappy.**

The Art Of Constructive Distraction

Use it. Anytime you feel the baby is tensing up or **thinking** about a maneuver, change the subject. Distraction can also mean performing the exercises so quickly — for a minute or two — that he doesn't have time to get upset. Be careful here though — don't overdo it. Temper your pace so that sometimes you are very fast with the exercise. (This could mean flipping five or six times in a minute.) Then, let the baby catch his breath while you radically change the pace and slow down to a snail's crawl. This changing of pace really keeps a baby on his toes! Distract his mind while you condition his body to adjust to new feelings. It keeps the lessons interesting.

I remember teaching a baby who refused to be distracted; he wanted his mommy and he wanted out — not necessarily in that order! I started fooling around with the pool filter, looking for dead leaves to ooh and ahh about, rubber toys, bugs, anything to catch his interest. I was holding the baby in one arm and digging into the pool filter with the other hand. As I was blindly dragging little goodies out, I latched onto a dead and bloated frog — the ugliest thing I have ever seen. I screamed, dropped the frog, and very nearly dropped the baby! But that touched his button. He giggled and chortled through the rest of the day. **Point to remember:** It is often the case that when you break the repetitions with a rest and try that same exercise later, the baby will do better!

"Get Back On The Horse"

These lessons are structured to minimize any fear. Few babies are frightened by this technique. But if there has been an occasion for the baby to get scared, it's awfully important for him to be re-exposed to the water soon after the experience.

I was bucked off a horse once as a child. I had all the wind knocked out of me and I was petrified. My father put me right back on the horse a few minutes later. If he hadn't put me back on, I would never have gone near a horse again as long as I lived. That goes double with scary water experiences.

Many adults who have never learned to swim usually have a childhood experience tucked away in their minds, an experience they were never helped to overcome **at the time.** Such traumas are only important if they are allowed to be buried and ignored, because the seed is planted and the fear grows. Facing the problem **erases** the problem.

The End Of Day Three

If the baby is old enough to stand up alone, let him swim out of the pool under his own power. Don't carry him out any more. After all, you won't be there to carry him out if he should fall in! Remember, the whole purpose of teaching your child to swim is to enable him to survive in the water without you. Send the baby to the steps the same way you send him to another person. At first, he may not know what to do when he gets to the steps, so give him a hand; but let him do most of it by himself. You will soon discover throughout these lessons that each time you send your waterbug to the steps, he'll get the idea that it's time to get out! **Point to remember:** When the baby climbs out of the pool his feet are wet and the pool siding is slippery. Be there to catch him if he slips. And **bravo! The hardest day is behind you!**

It will be important that you get the baby in the water later today, even if only for a few minutes. It's been a big day for lessons and you need to offset it with some playing time.

Swimming to the steps . . .

. . . and crawling out.

DAY THREE SUMMARY

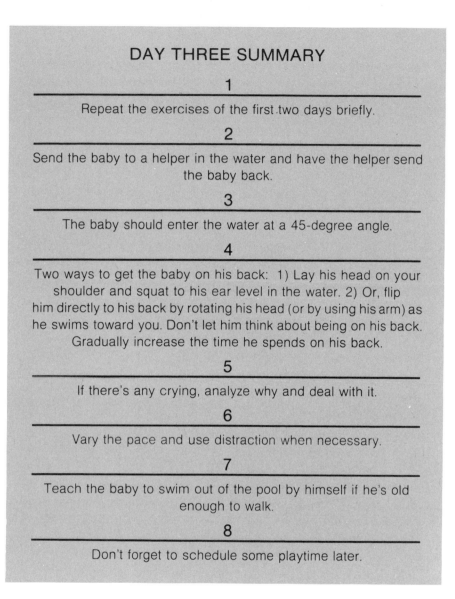

1

Repeat the exercises of the first two days briefly.

2

Send the baby to a helper in the water and have the helper send the baby back.

3

The baby should enter the water at a 45-degree angle.

4

Two ways to get the baby on his back: 1) Lay his head on your shoulder and squat to his ear level in the water. 2) Or, flip him directly to his back by rotating his head (or by using his arm) as he swims toward you. Don't let him think about being on his back. Gradually increase the time he spends on his back.

5

If there's any crying, analyze why and deal with it.

6

Vary the pace and use distraction when necessary.

7

Teach the baby to swim out of the pool by himself if he's old enough to walk.

8

Don't forget to schedule some playtime later.

DAY 4

The Flip

These last three days will be almost exclusively concerned with getting the baby to flip and float on his back by himself. This means a lot of reinforcement, pacing to avoid monotony with the repetitions, practice, and playtimes.

This half of the series can be very exciting. Somewhere in these next few days, the baby will suddenly catch on to what you've been teaching him. Until that happens, you may begin to think he will never get the idea of flipping on his own. Take heart, though, for in this chapter you will learn of the "Plateau Performer." Then, suddenly, your efforts will pay off: your little swimmer will surprise you with a startling performance.

Review Days One, Two And Three

You've heard it before: warm up with the previous days' work and then we will proceed with the new stuff. Start with swishing and pulling from the steps, season with happy talk and cuddles, mix in some handy distractions, and sprinkle with kisses. Now you're ready to cook up today's lesson.

Back With Balance

Yesterday you introduced the baby to the sensation of lying on his back. Today he should become more familiar with that position, and perhaps comfortable enough to acquire a sense of balance while on his back. He may now even float by himself! That will be accomplished by reducing the support he gets from your hands.

From the steps, pull the baby under water toward you. Keeping him at arm's length, slowly and gently rotate his head with your hands until he has flipped over to his back. Be sure you are blocking the sun from the baby's eyes with your shadow. Both your hands should be holding the baby's head ear-deep in the water.

You may find that the baby is still a bit nervous about this position, so talk to him. Stroke his face with one hand while holding his head with the other. Bend over and kiss his cheek, and then pick him up. Repeat this procedure over and over again, each time increasing the length of time the baby remains on his back.

Be alert as you flip the baby onto his back. Watch his mouth: if it's open as you turn him over, there will be water in it. If he has a mouthful of water and he's on his back, he could choke on it. Be prepared to raise the baby's head enough for him to clear his mouth and throat. **Note:** Raise his head for a moment, don't pick him up! We don't want to condition the baby into thinking that every time he gets water in his mouth he needs help!

If the baby coughs or sputters uncontrollably, of course, pick him up. No need to allow that kind of discomfort to occur while the child is on his back. If all has gone well and the baby is really quite used to lying there on his back, it's time to eliminate some of the support he has been getting from you.

Everything You Need To Know About Fingertip Control

After you turn the baby onto his back this time, very slowly remove one hand, holding the baby's head with the other. Caress his face, distracting him from what's going on under the water. Slowly drop part of your hand away from beneath his head, supporting him now only with your fingertips.

Let your fingertips do the work of your whole hand.

You will see the importance of maintaining the baby's head and body in a level position. If you have been holding the baby's head up too high, rather than allowing the water to maintain a natural buoyancy around him, his head will drop when you eliminate some support. There's nothing sneaky about eliminating support if the baby feels his head drop lower in the water.

Now that your fingertips are touching the back of the baby's head, start strumming your fingers on it. Try supporting him now with only two fingertips, then one — get the picture? The baby won't know how much you're helping and how much he's doing a balancing act on his own. Very gently, try dropping your fingertips away from the baby's head altogether. How long can he float by himself under the delusion that you are still supporting him?

As soon as the baby starts getting wise, or begins to lose his balance, put your hand back under his head. Stroke his face, give him hugs and kisses and try it again. **Don't stop talking to him.** Let him believe that as long as you are talking to him you are supporting him. Use your wits to distract the baby from what your hand is doing.

The Baby's Hands Can Help, Too

Keep the baby's hands busy. If his arms are active, he could throw himself off his delicate balance. Grasp both the baby's hands and place them under his head. This serves several purposes. First, it gives him something to do with his hands. Second, it helps the baby maintain a good floating position by helping counterbalance his legs, which sometimes tend to pull him down. And third, it helps disguise the fact that your hands are not under his head.

If the baby resists this position for now, put a toy in his hand. Just holding onto **something** helps relieve a lot of tension. If the toy doesn't work, let him hold your finger, but get those arms of his steady and quiet.

Keep Your Hands To Yourself!

Gently take away all your support and **keep talking**. The baby could float there by himself for minutes and minutes without knowing what he's doing. **But don't let the baby see your hands!** It could give the secret away. Remember, he's no dummy! If he happens to turn his head because he catches a glimpse of your hands moving out of the corner of his eye, he could lose his balance and all his glorious dignity and roll, feet first, under the water. He could scare himself. He's not in complete control yet!

Don't wait for him to lose his balance before you pick him up. Reward him for doing things right by picking him up. If you pick him up **after he loses his balance**, you only reward him for failing.

More Flipping More Often

We are very close to our goal. The baby should be able to float freely for short periods of time on his own. Now we want to extend that time and increase the child's ability to **flip** on his own. I have found that when a child begins to master the balance of floating, he is also capable **at the same time** of flipping on his own.

Wrong! Don't let the baby see your hands—he'll lose his balance reaching for you.

Just as you gradually eliminated support from the baby's head to get him floating, so you must gradually eliminate the help you give the child as he flips from his stomach to his back. As the baby swims toward you, turn his head, **but only three-quarters of the way**. Watch the baby work to complete the **feeling** or **habit** of turning all the way over to his back, since he's done this movement so many times before. Repeat this partial assistance several times. Eventually you will find yourself simply touching the baby's head under water and this will cue a reflex from the child to flip completely over on his own.

You'll remember that the alternate way of flipping the baby onto his back was by reaching for the baby's arm. Eliminating support by quarter turns will bring the same effect as turning his head in partial turns.

Be patient. It takes time and repetition.

What If He Doesn't Flip?

Don't be impatient. After all, this is only Day Four, not Day Six! Let's gradually allow the baby to remain under water for longer periods of time, until he realizes that if he wants to breathe, he **has to** flip. Obviously, you must not push this last step too far too fast. I have had babies who would rather turn blue in the face before they would turn on their own when they were perfectly capable of doing so! Babies can be terribly stubborn sometimes and seem to resent the notion of doing anything for themselves. Remember, no one has ever made the baby do anything on his own before. He hasn't been forced to eat anything he doesn't want to eat. He doesn't have to change his clothes, clean his room, or excuse himself to go to the bathroom! He has existed completely on a dependent and nurturing system up to now. This is the first time that the notion of independence has been presented to him. So be patient if you find that at first the baby isn't willing to give up "the good life" and accept responsibility. You may find yourself stuck at this learning point — it's called a "plateau."

Plateau Performers

Every dieter knows what a plateau is. A "plateau performer" is that man, woman or child who attempts to reach a goal and all of a sudden finds himself making no progress. He even seems to be getting worse instead of better.

You may find that after four days of amazing progress, the baby suddenly seems to forget what he learned just the day before, for no apparent reason! Don't panic, don't push and don't give up! **The baby is starting to think.** He has absorbed so much information that he needs time now to digest it all. If the baby is allowed the time he needs, he will suddenly begin the upward climb toward the watersafe goal. He is on the verge of discovering a form of complete and undeniable autonomy, thanks to your patience and understanding. Plateaus are necessary to learning.

Remember Games and Distractions!

You will find yourself spending the entire lesson simply repeating turns, eliminating support, over and over and — BLAH! — over again. Repetition is the key, so hang in there. But make it fun. Conjure up games and distractions in between.

Swimming to the Side

Depending on how big and strong the baby is, his learning how to swim to the side of the pool can be a valuable bit of knowledge.

Check the level of the water in the pool. It has to be high enough so that when the little swimmer comes to the side, it takes little effort for him to reach up and out of the water, grab onto the edge of the pool, and breathe!

Begin by sending the baby to the side of the pool the same way you scoot him to the steps. Follow him to the side after you let go of him and give his bottom a nudge. Then help him lift his hand up to the edge. Naturally, you wouldn't expect a very small infant to be able to do this, but if he is crawling or walking, chances are he is also strong enough to hang on to the poolside.

Wrong Again, Charley

You might run into a little problem with a baby who insists on turning around **under** the water and swimming back to you, rather than grabbing onto the side and helping himself out.

If you pick him up when he swims back to you, you are, in effect, telling him that you will always be there to help him out. You are telling him that if he doesn't want to handle the job, he doesn't have to. Well, wrong again, Charley!

Swimming to the side . . .

If your baby swims back to you, swing him around back to the side, raising his hand up to the side to give him the idea. If he still tries to turn around to you, be firm and again push him back to the side of the pool. He's probably running short of breath by this time, so be sure that when he gets to the side with your guidance, he surfaces for air the way you want him to, hanging

onto the edge of the pool. Four or five repetitions of this exercise should get the idea across.

. . . reaching up and holding on.

Playtime

Today's lesson should last no more than half an hour. The baby can get very tired since the lessons are demanding, but he still needs some time to play in the water several hours after he's napped and is refreshed. **Playtime is as important as the lessons. Do not overlook it!**

DAY FOUR SUMMARY

1

Review the previous day's work.

2

Reduce the support you give the baby on his back while increasing the length of time he stays on his back.

3

Reduce support by using "fingertip control." How long can he float by himself under the assumption that you are holding him up? Even a few seconds count!

4

Take a hint from the magician. Don't show your hands and give the secret away. You could distract him and cause him to lose his orientation and his trust in you.

5

If the baby is learning to float on his own, he is also ready to flip on his own. Begin by initiating the flip and allow the baby to complete it. This won't be accomplished all in one day, so be patient.

6

Repetition is the key to everything, but remember to intersperse the repetitions with play and exciting distractions.

7

Depending on the age, size, and development of the baby, teaching him to swim to the poolside and to reach his hand out to the edge is a good diversion from routine. It's also a way for the baby to keep himself alive if he should fall into the pool. Scoot him to the side and pull his hand up to the edge, time and time again, until he catches on to the idea.

Continued/

8

If the baby swims back to you rather than the poolside, turn him back toward it. The urge to breathe will encourage him to be attentive.

9

We are all plateau performers. If the baby regresses, or appears to forget even the simplest of things, he is still learning but in a different way. He is assimilating the knowledge and use of his newly acquired skills. Give him time and patience. Don't push, but don't quit either. Keep practicing. Keep repeating!

DAY 5

Flipping and Floating

Today we are going to give the baby more opportunity to be in control. On Day Five your little swimmer will be expected to swim toward you under water, flip over on his own to his back, and, finally, float on his own. It sounds like a lot to expect today; but if the plateau is wearing off or if you've been lucky enough not to hit that snag, today could be **the day** it all comes together.

Begin with the usual review of the last four days before taking the next step.

Why Should I?

The baby must have an incentive for turning to his back or he just won't cooperate — why should he? You're always there helping out, and he understands only that. The key then is to allow the baby to make up his own mind — to determine for himself when and why he should flip. The answer is simple: he needs to breathe.

By now you have a handle on how long the baby can swim under water without needing a breath. Extend that time slightly. Allow him the **experience** of needing a breath, and then help him over to his back by turning his head or by flipping him with his arm. If you let him get slightly out of breath under water, he'll get the message. He'll be glad to be on his back, where he's able to see you, breathe the sweet air and relax.

The very moment the baby flips to his back and takes a gasp of air, gently but quickly remove your support. He will be so busy catching his breath that he won't have time to notice your hands are not holding him up! This is an example of distraction at work.

Now obviously we are not out to scare the baby or to worry him in any way, so don't overreact to this part of the lesson. My intention is not to have him gulping and gasping for air while you stand idly by. By all means, help him out! Don't wait for him to turn blue in the face. Put yourself in his position for a moment. You are under water, you begin to feel the need for air and you surface. It is precisely the feeling of "I think I'd better go up for air now" that we want the baby to experience. Allow him that experience. Allow him that discovery. You won't hurt him. You won't scare him. Let him discover for himself that the air is where his back is!

Spend most of this lesson repeating, repeating, repeating.

If He Hates Being On His Back

The back float is often an uncomfortable and vulnerable position for the baby at first. Few children naturally sleep on their backs. In fact, most mothers place their children on their stomach in the crib for fear the child might choke on its back. This is a conditioning, a direct message to the baby that his back is taboo. So don't be surprised if the child tends to struggle with the back float position or has difficulty accepting it.

If your baby is really outraged with the idea, think for a moment about what you might have done in the past to make him resent it. Do you wash your baby's hair in the bathtub, forcing him to lie backwards as you pour water over his head? He could be carrying that feeling to the pool with him. Many babies don't like that feeling. (It is often better to wash the child's head at home by having him lie on the kitchen counter, on dry ground, with only his head over the sink. That way, he won't equate water in the pool with hair-washing and hair-raising experiences!)

If the baby is crying while he's on his back, he's telling you he's insecure with the sensation. The only way to build his confidence in that position is to put him back on that proverbial horse! Put him back on his back. Repeat it over and over and over again.

Most importantly, don't give in to yelling and screaming. If the baby is making a lot of noise, continue speaking softly and wait out his temper tantrum. You may find that by whispering to him he will settle down in order to hear you. Whispers keep potential screamers down to an audible roar — sometimes.

One more thought: not all babies cry. We speak of it because we want to cover all the bases. But if the crying disturbs you, what would disturb you more, a few tears now or a tragedy later? The tears won't last — remember that. They pass and the baby will not dwell on them. His string of little victories during this series will wash all tears away. Our years of teaching have proved this to be true.

Losing His Balance — And Other Problems

The baby **will** lose his balance on his back — that's what learning is all about! He'll roll over to a face-down position from time to time while he learns to balance himself. That's okay! Only through knowing his mistakes and how to correct them will the baby be able to judge which way is up! Once you have the baby on his back and you release your support, he may wobble a bit and may even lose his balance altogether and flip to his tummy. We didn't allow this to happen on Day Four or Day Three. We supported him (for the most part), not asking him to balance by himself on those days. But today we will allow him, on his own, to **lose** his balance, which will help him discover **how** to balance. When the baby flips to his face-down position, count to four or five before helping him flip right side up again. The five count gives him time to adjust to where he is and why.

Overarching

Some babies may overcompensate for their balance on their backs by arching too much and forcing their heads back too far. This usually happens when you have reduced your support from under his head too fast. The urge for the baby then is to push his head back under water, "looking" for those hands of yours that were supposed to be there. The tendency to overarch is also a nervous reaction to his lack of confidence

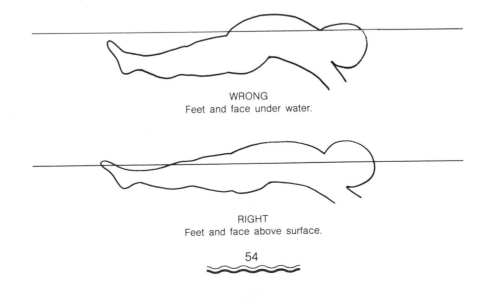

WRONG
Feet and face under water.

RIGHT
Feet and face above surface.

and his inability to handle the task before him. In this case, the baby will require a lot of patience and a lot of back resting. Place the baby on his back, his head cupped in your hands, and have him lie there for up to ten minutes. You may sit on the steps and talk to the infant, stroking his head and generally restoring his confidence. Many times I've had babies fall asleep in this position — that's how comfortable they became! Remember, water is soothing, and if the baby is allowed to lie quietly on his back he could drift off into sweet slumber. Good! He's obviously relaxed. Then try reducing your support again.

Waving Hands

It's a good idea to get the baby's hands behind his head. This keeps them busy and aids in float control. If he insists on waving them around in the air, give him a toy to hold on to, as we discussed earlier. Or, let him hold your finger or his hair. Usually, by grasping something babies feel more secure and get a sense of being "grounded."

The Toss

The hell you say! Well, you know, the baby is not going to fall into the water on a gentle breath-cue. When he goes, he's going to go! Splash! Noise! Depth! Bubbles! The works! The dog may brush against him at poolside and knock him in with little ceremony. So it's time to teach the baby how to handle a potential **panic situation**. Let's get him used to the feeling of falling from a little height (and all the commotion that goes with it) so that when it does happen for real, the baby treats the situation with a ho-hum attitude rather than sheer fright and paralysis. Believe me, this is a gentle and even fun thing for the baby. Yet to an unaccustomed eye it may look a bit bizarre. But have faith. You will discover that the baby will treat the entire thing with a giggle or a shrug.

When you pull your baby from the side of the pool, he falls about a foot. The only difference now is that he won't be sitting on the side. He's in your arms instead. Quickly raise the baby up, in any position, in any direction and let him drop in the water. Remember, when he falls for real, he's not going to fall in any proper fashion, so it doesn't matter **how** he enters the water. What's important is how he gets out of it!

If you've done your work properly these past five days, the baby will pop up to the surface like a little cork and, quite complacently, flip to his back! Don't rush him; give him time. Don't try helping him out, like yanking him up from the depths before his buoyancy does it for him. That would cause more

distress than it would help him. As patiently as you can, stand back and watch the baby work things out for himself. One day, when it happens for real, you won't be there to help. We are simulating that experience now. When the baby comes to the surface, if he doesn't flip over then give him a hand. You know now what part to work on with him, but chances are good that the baby will amaze you and react to the toss with composure and aplomb!

Repeat the toss several times, each time tossing the baby a little higher into the air.

We've had so many babies who really enjoy this part of the lessons more than any other. Some parents play a game of "ball" with the waterbug, tossing him from one to the other, and the baby really loves it!

The toss: starting high . . .

. . . dropping hands away . . . and baby goes in head first . . .

. . . he begins his flip . . . **important**—give him time to try!

Mission accomplished.

Can A Splash Hurt?

Some parents ask if the splash will hurt the baby — sting him like a belly flop. The answer is no. The baby is very light and is being tossed from arm's length only, so there's not really much force to the fall. Besides, if it does sting, don't you think the baby will let you know it?

We are talking about **tossing** the baby into the water, not throwing him — there is a difference. Don't thrust him **down** into the water but gently toss him **up**. I would not recommend the toss for infants under five months old since they require a more gentle hand.

One last word on the toss: don't confuse this with any "sink or swim" methods you've heard about. If you have followed through with the last five days, you must surely appreciate the fact that this is the second to last day of the training lessons, not the first. We are reasonably sure that the baby can handle this situation or we wouldn't have proceeded to this point. The toss and the subsequent graduation tests are the **results** of his lessons, not the **means** by which he was taught.

DAY FIVE SUMMARY

1

Day Five is repetition and more repetition: flipping over to the back, learning to balance, and swimming under water for longer periods of time.

2

To show the baby the reason for being on his back, allow him to run short of air before helping him onto his back. Continue to decrease support.

3

Don't give in to any tearful resistance; be firm, be calm, but be gentle.

4

To acquaint the baby with the splashing that accompanies an accidental fall into the water, toss him in the air, let him splash, and allow him to surface as his own buoyance takes over. Then help him to his back.

5

Allow the baby to float on his back for minutes at a time. This position should become second nature to him now.

6

If you run into problems such as overarching or kicking, read up on the sections dealing with those problems. Patience and repetition are usually the clues to working them out.

7

Don't forget a playtime later in the day.

DAY 6

Graduation

Today is the big day—today is the day everybody has been working toward. Today is the day the baby gets to show off his flipping and floating talents for all the world to see. And this is **polish-up** day, when all the rough edges get rounded out. Take it nice and easy.

Reinforcement

You should be good at this by now. If the baby doesn't yet swim an appreciable distance under water, work on that. I say appreciable because every baby is different. You'll have to use your own judgment. Usually, a baby can swim at least a yard before flipping over. Most of my babies have been able to do one width of the pool. (That's with help from me, in creating a wake or current that they can easily swim into.) A child of six months or older can manage that distance quite comfortably. If that is not the case with your little swimmer, don't fret. It will happen in his own good time.

If flipping is still a problem, go back to days Two and Three; brush up on quick, rapid-fire flips. Do about eight flips helping the baby and then see if he doesn't pick up on it himself by flip number nine. When you suddenly aren't there to help him get over, he will be forced to do it himself. He may be expecting another quick flip with help from you, but without knowing it he's done the job on his own.

If the baby is wobbly on his back, let him float around the pool for several minutes. Sometimes I have put the baby on his back and slipped out of the water for a cup of coffee at poolside. The baby just merrily floats around the pool like a little waterbug for up to ten or fifteen minutes, until I climb back in the pool and pick him up!

Graduation Test

Do not attempt this final test unless you are reasonably sure that the baby can handle the responsibility.

If all has gone well up to this point, we are ready to graduate the baby to the fullest possible degree of his ability. We must know for sure if he will react as taught to an unexpected problem—that of being unbalanced and flung into the water without warning. Now remember, this is a **simulation** of a possible accident—a drill! If he **does** have a problem you will be there to help him out—this time. But for the most part, it's all up to the baby today. This is a drill for the purpose of reinforcing, practicing, and correcting any possible problems now, rather than finding out what he didn't know later, when it may be too late.

Take the baby out of the pool and dry him off a little. Then, very casually, start walking around the pool's deck, up to the pool's edge. Gently tumble the baby into the water. Watch closely — he should pop up to the surface and flip to his back just as he did during the tossing exercises. This will not hurt the baby. This will not scare him either, since he is more than prepared to handle the problem. That has been the purpose of these last six days.

Simulating an accidental fall

Don't be afraid to let go!

She passes the test with flying colors.

Once the baby has flipped to his back, cheer him on with praise: "Oh, good boy! I'm so proud of you!" Allow him to lie out there for a while — he should be able to float on his back indefinitely.

Perform the test a few more times.

"What If He Didn't Pass?" — A Word on Expectations

Do you throw in the towel in despair? Do you relegate your baby to the "dummy class" for the rest of his natural life? Of course not. We have progressed very quickly in just six short days. If there is a problem, the baby just needs a little more time. Not **everyone** can be expected to be a Six Day Wonder. Your child is no dummy just because he didn't live up to your expectations. Remember, Einstein flunked algebra in high school! The baby could surprise you tomorrow. If the baby is a gem and a hypothetically perfect student, you do have a Six Day Wonder Bunny on your hands. Ninety percent of the children we teach have proved adept at water survival in six days. We just don't want you feeling that your baby is a failure if he isn't quite there yet. Sometimes a few days' break from the lessons will do miracles. Relax the expectations and do a lot of playing. In a couple of days, try again.

Follow Up

Just because the sixth day has finally arrived and your baby has accomplished all that you set out to teach him, remember — his learning has just begun! Now you must set out a continuous program of reinforcement and experimentation with the baby. Go through the drills with him at least once a week. That includes lots of swimming, lots of flipping and floating and, every now and then, a friendly shove when the baby least expects it. Be sure he remembers how to react to unexpected events. This way, forgetting is impossible.

What Next?

While everybody is busy patting himself on the back, most of the progress the baby makes from this point will be on his own terms and on his own time. He will not remain at this static stage of simply flipping and floating. He will get bored with that after a time and as his sense of independence grows, so will his need for experimenting. Gradually he will begin to try other things, like swimming a little further or jumping to you on his own from the steps or even from the diving board! (Let's hope you have a strong heart!) You may even notice the baby starting a sort of bobbing action for air, up on his back for a breath and then back under to swim. He's on his way to rhythmic breathing and soon the standard crawl stroke. Your little peanut will amaze you with all the terrific feats he will pull off — if you let him, by making his swimming a joyful and experimental experience.

I remember one little 14-month-old girl who really went bananas with experimenting. She was flipping and floating like a real champ when I left her. Two weeks after the lessons, I got a frantic call from her mother. She said she was at the end of her rope and that no punishment seemed to work. The baby was doing flips and somersaults off the diving board! She didn't think the baby was supposed to do that yet! I was pleasantly surprised that a 14-month-old should be doing so well! The baby was safe, happy, and having a ball. The only problem was that she was learning so fast her mother couldn't keep up with her!

DAY SIX SUMMARY

1
Work on the rough edges today.

2
If you are reasonably sure that the baby can handle the responsibility of the graduation test, toss him in the water from the pool's edge. Allow him time to surface, flip, and float on his own.

3
If the baby's performance does not meet your expectations, lay off the lessons for a few days and try later. That usually does the trick.

4
Continue the drills about once a week. Remember, playing is just as important as practice.

5
Allow the baby to experiment with his newfound freedoms in the water. He will grow into new abilities very fast.

6
Have a cool drink and relax — your baby is water-safe and you're a fine instructor.

A watersafe graduate!

Diploma

This document certifies that

_____

graduated with distinction

from the six-day

watersafe training course

on

_____, 198__

Witness:

_____

APPENDIX

Older Babies and Games

What About Older Babies

Obviously, the older your baby, the more you'll have to reason with him. You will have to be able to tell a two or three-year-old **why** you want him to do the things you want him to do! There are many different little games you can play to get the same results but there are not many differences with the technique itself.

Day One is the same, introducing the baby to the water gradually, although the older child can stand on the steps and get himself wet: a kneecap, a belly button and a chin at a time. After he's happy with being wet, take him in your arms and swish him the way you would a smaller child, but give him more frequent rest breaks than with an infant because older children are more likely to think things through and reflect. A baby, on the other hand, is more likely to react to situations **at the moment**. You must take things at a slower pace with an older child since it's easier to frighten him. That's why teaching an infant to swim at a very early stage in his little life is so important!

During the swishing and "going under" stages of the first day, act quickly but do the exercises less often. Pretend not to notice that the little one went under. If you are neutral about this experience, chances are he will be neutral about it. After you put the tot under water the first time, immediately do something else. Play with a toy, put him back on the steps, look for fish, or distract him in some other way.

A little later, with a quick movement and the baby an arm's distance away, swish him sideways and under water again. Repeat this procedure a few times until he's fairly comfortable with the underwater feeling.

Teaching a young tot to hold his breath is the biggest hurdle. Once he is able to accomplish this task, the rest of the lesson plan is easy and routine, except for the games you'll have to play.

Names of the Games

This teaching method is as much a psychological technique as it is a physical one. When working with older kids, you will have to develop a superb sense of gamesmanship. A good game to teach a tot breath holding is to take advantage of his capitalistic little heart — pennies! This is a good Day Two game.

Come to the pool with a provocative handful of bright copper pennies. Sitting on the steps, put a few pennies on the first step. Tell the tot that he can **keep** all the pennies he can get! Well, that's easy, he only needs to reach down and the pennies are his. But now, after you've perked his interest in this game, place a few pennies on the second step. Usually, the coins are just outside a comfortable arm's reach. In order to get them, the tot will have to squat. This means getting his chin wet or maybe even his lips! If you apply the right kind of encouragement, you may find the child is willing to put his face in the water for just a second to get hold of the penny. You can offer your help by directing his hand or showing him how to do it.

This game is effective, but play it only **after** you've exposed him to the underwater swishes from Day One. A big advantage of this game is that you are giving the older child a chance to be in control, to make his own decisions as to **when** he's ready to put his face in. This works…sometimes. At other times, the tot will only stall and will obviously not try to do this exercise on his own. In this event, take the child in your arms and try an underwater swish before returning him to the steps. You may find that he will prefer doing it on his own, rather than have you swish him. Give him the choice, "You do it by yourself, or I'll have to help you." A great tactic, and it usually works. If the child simply won't respond to this, do some more swishing as you would with an infant in Day One and Two.

Rings and Things

This is a great Day Three game. Most drug stores and pool supply stores carry brightly colored underwater rings and other toys that sink. On Day Three, when you are exposing your little two or three-year-old to being under water for longer periods of time, it helps to have a reason to be under there! Grabbing colored rings could be just the thing!

Holding the child the same way you would an infant on the third day (at a 45-degree angle to the water, stretched over your arms), dive him down and help him grab a ring. The pride of the accomplishment should be more thrilling than the fact that he went under. In many cases, children are so concerned with whether or not they got the ring, they completely overlook the fact that they were under at all! And this all depends on your skill as an instructor to distract him from that point.

How Long Can You Hold Your Breath?

With some youngsters, you'll find yourself in a very philosophical discussion on breath holding. Three-year-olds are great talkers, and they would rather **talk** than swim in the initial stages of the lessons. So take advantage of his verbosity! How long can you hold your breath? Very magnanimously and dramatically inhale and puff up your cheeks, holding your breath. Then, just as dramatically, exhale. Then ask chatterbox to do the same. In a follow-the-leader manner, cup a little water in your hands, take that great big breath and put your mouth in the water. Ask your charge to do the same. Then it's simple, "See, we're holding our breath under water!"

Now, if this is all working for you, the next step is placing your lips at water level and having the tot do the same, eventually going to the penny game.

Another Breath Holding Trick

Wipe and blow! Make that a password to underwater work. Sometimes little ones will come up from the water wide eyed, rubbing their eyes or asking for a towel. Show the child how to wipe his face with a downward stroke of his hand, blowing the water out of his mouth at the same time. This is the magic trick. (Children just love magic tricks and if you tell them that there's a magic trick to getting the water off their faces, they'll buy it.) Wipe and blow! Abracadabra, the water is gone!

Blowing Bubbles

Yes, friends, another trick. Getting a baby's face wet is a big trick, even trickier is doing it without his knowing it! An older child can be "persuaded" that a wet face is okay if you play the blowing and kicking game. Now, we usually discourage kicking in these lessons, but we'll resort to anything when it comes to trickery.

Have the child lay down on the top steps on his tummy, blowing **loud** bubbles in the water and kicking his legs at the same time. Be there next to him doing the same thing. After he's into the exercise and isn't noticing you, use a hand to slosh water over him. Keep your kicking up so that the water is turbulent enough to splash on his cheeks. The back of his head and his face should be thoroughly wet while the little guy is still busy trying to blow those loud bubbles for you and is still kicking furiously. This is also a handy warm-up exercise in case the child gets chilly!

You will no doubt find your own little games that work with your baby's emotional chemistry. Use games with older children at every opportunity but don't become so engrossed with the game that you lose sight of the reason for it! If you are not accomplishing a constructive result with the game during the lesson, then resort back to the drills or think of another way to get the same thing accomplished. Don't spend all the lesson time trying to talk the tot into seeing things your way. If at first you don't succeed, go to the drills as outlined in the first part of this book. Each day something constructive **must** be accomplished before drying-off time.

B

Safety and Life Support

The publisher recommends that all parents who are interested in pro-
moting water activities with their children take the basic water safety and
CPR courses offered by local organizations such as the American Red
Cross. The following information has been supplied by the American Red
Cross and the American Heart Association for reference in the event of an
emergency.

Artificial Respiration

A respiratory emergency is an emergency in which normal breathing stops
or in which breathing is so reduced that oxygen intake is insufficient to support life. The average person may die in 6 minutes or less if his oxygen supply
is cut off. Since it is often impossible to tell exactly when a person has
stopped breathing, artificial respiration should be started as rapidly as
possible. The mouth-to-mouth technique of artificial respiration is the
most practical and effective method for emergency ventilation of a
person of any age who has stopped breathing. When breathing stops, you
should quickly proceed as follows:

1. If a victim appears to be unconscious, tap him on the shoulder and
   shout, "Are you okay?" (Fig. A).

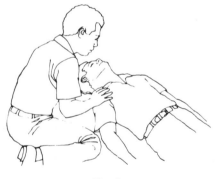

Fig. A

2. If there is no response, tilt the victim's head, chin pointing up. Place
   one hand under the victim's neck and gently lift. At the same time,
   push with the other hand on the victim's forehead (Fig. B). This will
   move the tongue away from the back of the throat to open the airway.

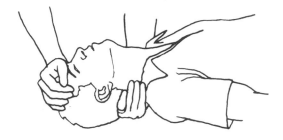

Fig. B

Immediately look, listen, and feel for air (Fig. C). While maintaining the backward head tilt position, place your cheek and ear close to the victim's mouth and nose. Look for the chest to rise and fall while you listen and feel for the return of air. Check for about 5 seconds.

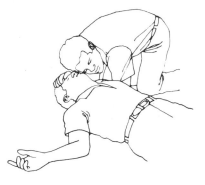

Fig. C

3. If the victim is not breathing, give four quick breaths.
   - Maintain the backward head tilt.
   - Pinch the victim's nose with the hand that is on the victim's forehead to prevent leakage of air.
   - Open your mouth wide, take a deep breath, seal your mouth around the victim's mouth, and blow into the victim's mouth with four quick but full breaths just as fast as you can (Fig. D). Use only enough time between breaths to lift your head slightly for better inhalation.

Fig. D

- **FOR AN INFANT**, give gentle puffs, blow through the mouth **and** nose, and do not tilt the head back as far as for an adult.
- If you do not get an air exchange when you blow, it may help to re-position the head and try again.
  LOOK, LISTEN, AND FEEL FOR AIR EXCHANGE (Fig. E).

Fig. E

4. If there is still no breathing, change rate to one breath every 5 seconds for an adult (Figs. F and G).
   FOR AN INFANT, give one gentle puff every 3 seconds.

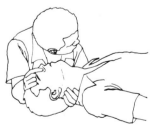

Fig. F   Fig. G

5. The mouth-to-nose method can be used with the sequence described above instead of the mouth-to-mouth method. Maintain the backward-head-tilt position with the hand on the victim's forehead. Remove the hand from under the neck and close the victim's mouth. Blow into the victim's nose (Fig. H). Open the victim's mouth for the look, listen and feel step (Fig. I).

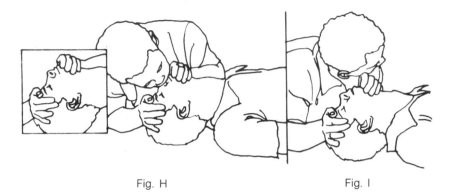

Fig. H   Fig. I

6. In administering artificial respiration to a **SMALL CHILD**, you should seal off both the mouth and nose of the infant with your mouth (Fig. J). Blow into the child's mouth and nose every 3 seconds (about 20 breaths per minute) with less pressure and volume than used for an adult, the amount determined by the size of the child. Only small puffs of air will suffice for infants.

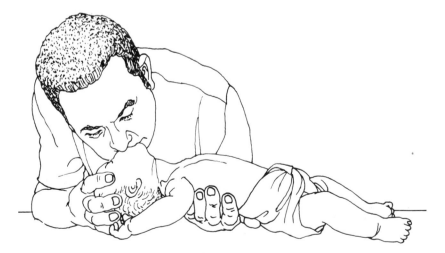

Fig. J

Because a respiratory emergency necessitates immediate action, it may be necessary to administer artificial respiration initially in the water. Although this procedure is extremely difficult in deep water, even for a skilled swimmer using flotation devices, it can be done with relative ease in water of standing depth (Fig. K). The buoyancy of the victim's body provides support, and the rescuer maintains the victim's head position and administers mouth-to-mouth respiration as on land. Artificial respiration may also be administered while afloat in small craft, and if the distance to shore is great, it would certainly be advisable to begin this procedure while hanging onto the boat as you would a pool side (Fig. L).

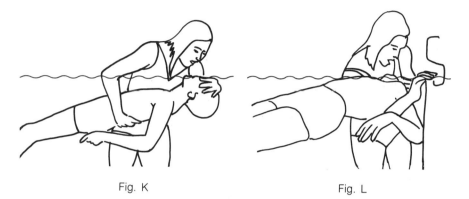

Fig. K   Fig. L

For more information about artificial respiration, refer to current first aid publications that are available from your Red Cross chapter.

Supplementary Care—Victims of near drownings must be given some supplementary care, including immediate treatment to prevent shock, followed by medical care. Supplementary care is as follows:

1. Treat for shock.
   - Keep the victim lying down.
   - Maintain body temperature.
2. Make sure that the victim is seen by a physician, to assure proper medical care.

—Excerpted from **Basic Rescue and Water Safety**, Second Edition, copyright 1974, 1980 by The American National Red Cross. Used with permission.

Basic Life Support in Infants and Children

The basic principles of CPR (cardiopulmonary resuscitation) are the same whether the victim is an infant, child, or adult. These principles include:

1. Establishing unresponsiveness or respiratory difficulty.
2. Calling for help.
3. Positioning the victim.
4. Airway: (a) Opening the airway; (b) Establishing breathlessness.
5. Breathing for the victim: (a) Rescue breathing; (b) Recognizing and managing the obstructed airway.
6. Circulation: (a) Establishing the presence or absence of pulse; (b) Activating the emergency medical services (EMS) system; (c) Applying external chest compression.

The differences in CPR in the infant and child are in priorities and techniques to allow for different underlying causes of the emergencies in infants and children and for variation in size.

Size of the Infant or Child — Children differ in size from infancy through adolescence. For the purpose of CPR, we have called anyone younger than 1 year an infant and between 1 and 8 years a child. Techniques appropriate to the adult may be applied to children older than 8 years of age. It is recognized that there are large infants (younger than 1 year of age) who might be mistaken for a child (1 to 8 years), while at the other end, a small adolescent might be mistaken for a child. These definitions should be taken as guidelines only. At the time of an emergency, one should not try to be too exact about age, since a slight error one way or the other is not critical.

Establishing Unresponsiveness or Respiratory Difficulty

An unconscious infant or child, like an adult, will not awaken or cry when shaken. The extremities will be limp. Therefore, to determine if an infant or child is unconscious, he should be gently tapped or shaken. If conscious, he will begin to move and cry.

If a child is not unconscious but is gasping and struggling to breathe, he may need to have his airway opened and, if necessary, have rescue breathing coordinated to his breathing. As previously noted, the need for rescue breathing is more commonly required in infants and children than in adults.

Positioning the Victim — The circumstances in which the child victim is found will determine to some degree the care that must be exercised in positioning him. The likelihood of neck, spine, or bone injuries will be greater if the victim is found at the scene of an accident or at the base of a tree than if an infant is found in bed not breathing. If the infant or child is face down, he must be rolled over as a unit. One hand should always support the head and neck so that it does not roll or twist.

The Airway

Opening the Airway — Once it has been established that the infant or child is unconscious or is having serious difficulty breathing, the airway should be opened. An infant or child who is struggling to breathe but whose color is not blue probably has an adequate airway and is best immediately transported by the rescuer to an ALS (advanced life support) facility. The infant or child who is not breathing or is making breathing efforts but is blue should have the airway opened. This is best done by the head tilt-neck lift technique or the head tilt augmented by the chin lift. The head tilt-neck lift technique is performed by placing one hand (or as many fingers as will fit comfortably) under the victim's neck and the other hand on the forehead (Fig. 1, upper right). The neck is lifted slightly and the head pushed back with gentle pressure on the forehead. This extension of the head will usually be sufficient to move the tongue away so it does not obstruct the airway. In some situations, the chin lift technique may be helpful in moving the tongue forward and away from the posterior pharyngeal wall. In this technique, extension of the head is maintained by pressure on the forehead. The tips of the fingers of the hand that had been under the neck are now used to lift the bony part of the jaw near the chin forward (Fig. 1, upper left). Care should be exercised that the mouth is not closed completely and that the fingers are not causing undue pressure on the soft tissue under the jaw.

Establishing Breathlessness—As soon as the airway is opened and while it is maintained, the rescuer should immediately check whether the victim is breathing. The rescuer places his ear over the victim's mouth and nose and looks toward the victim's chest and abdomen. The victim is breathing if the rescuer (1) sees the chest and abdomen rise and fall, (2) feels air from the mouth and nose, and (3) hears air during exhalation.

It should be stressed that the airway may be obstructed despite respiratory efforts by the victim. Often, opening the airway is all the victim needs to breathe effectively. If the victim resumes breathing, the airway is simply maintained. If the victim is not breathing, rescue breathing is applied. If after opening the airway the rescuer finds the infant or child is gasping or struggling to catch his breath, a decision has to be made by the rescuer whether to apply rescue breathing. This decision can be made by looking for blueness of the lips (the lips themselves, not the skin surrounding the lips), which is a sign of oxygen lack. If the lips are pink, enough oxygen is reaching the blood, and rescue breathing should not be attempted; instead, the victim should be transported as rapidly as possible to an ALS unit while patency of the airway is maintained. If the lips of an infant or child who is not breathing or who is struggling to breathe are blue, not enough oxygen is reaching the blood and rescue breathing is applied.

Breathing

Rescue breathing refers to the ventilation of a non-breathing infant, child, or adult by a rescuer. If the victim is an infant, the rescuer must cover both the mouth and the nose and make a seal. If the child is large enough so that a tight seal cannot be made over both nose and mouth together, the nose is pinched as in the adult, and only the mouth of the child is covered as in ventilation of the adult victim (Fig. 1, center panel).

When an airtight seal has been established—either mouth-to-nose and mouth, or mouth-to-mouth—four gentle breaths are delivered in rapid succession without allowing for full lung deflation. These four quick breaths serve as a means of checking for airway obstruction as well as opening the small air sacs in the lungs. The lungs of a child and especially an infant are smaller than those of an adult and have a correspondingly smaller volume. Ventilation should be limited to the amount of air needed to cause the chest to rise. It should not, however, be forgotten that the smaller air passages provide a greater resistance to air flow, and the rescuer's blowing pressure will probably have to be greater than he imagines. As soon as the chest, which should be carefully watched, is seen to rise and fall, the right amount of force is being used.

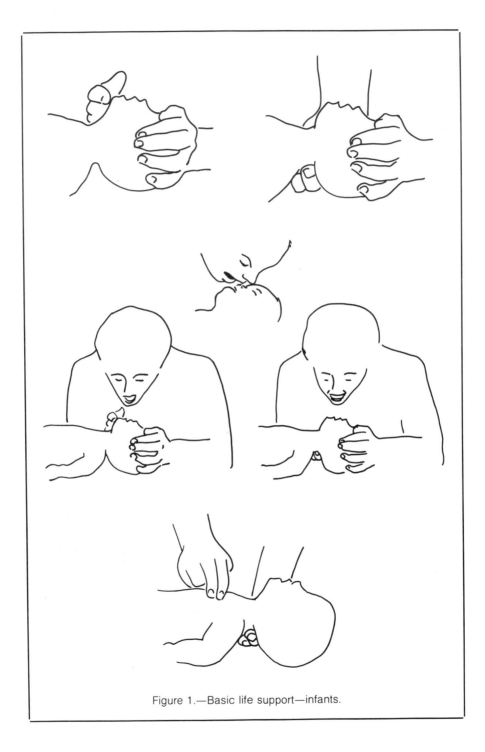

Figure 1.—Basic life support—infants.

If air enters freely with the four breaths and the chest rises, the airway is clear and the rescuer proceeds with checking the pulse. If air does not enter freely, patency of the airway should be checked. If, after readjustments of head extension and chin lift, air still does not enter freely, an obstruction must be suspected.

Gastric Distention—Artificial ventilation can cause stomach distention that, if excessive, can interfere with rescue breathing by elevating the diaphragm and thus decreasing lung volume. The incidence of gastric distention can be minimized by limiting ventilation volumes to the point at which the chest rises, thereby avoiding exceeding the esophageal opening pressure. Attempts at relieving gastric distention by pressure on the abdomen should be avoided because of the danger of aspirating stomach contents into the lungs. Gastric decompression should be attempted only if the abdomen is so tense that ventilation is ineffective. In such a situation, the infant's or child's entire body is turned to the side before pressure is applied to the abdomen.

Airway Obstruction—It should be kept in mind that airway obstruction with secondary cardiac arrest is much more common in infants and children than cardiac arrest with secondary airway obstruction. Airway obstruction can be caused by a foreign body such as a toy, peanut, or other small objects, or may be caused by an infection that causes swelling of the airway, such as occurs in croup or epiglottitis. The differentiation between a foreign body and an infectious cause is important, since in the latter case, going through the following steps for dislodging a foreign body will not be helpful, can be dangerous, and will cause delay in transporting the child to an appropriate ALS unit. The signs of croup or epiglottitis are those of airway obstruction, and the underlying cause can only be suspected at the time of an emergency by the circumstances under which the event occurred. A child who has been ill with fever, a barking cough, and progressive airway obstruction needs transportation to the nearest ALS facility, whereas a child, previously healthy, who chokes while eating peanuts or playing with small toys and has difficulty breathing may need CPR and relief of the airway obstruction. Foreign bodies may cause partial or complete airway obstruction. With partial airway obstruction, the victim may be capable of either good air exchange or poor air exchange. With good air exchange, the victim can cough forcefully, although there may be wheezing between the coughs. As long as good air exchange continues, the victim should be allowed and encouraged to persist with spontaneous coughing and breathing efforts. At this point, the rescuer should not interfere with the victim's attempts to expel the foreign body.

Poor air exchange may be present initially, or good air exchange may progress to poor air exchange. Poor air exchange is characterized by an ineffective cough, high-pitched noises while inhaling, increased respiratory difficulty, and especially blueness of the lips, nails, and skin. Partial obstruction with poor air exchange should be managed as a complete obstruction. Relief of foreign-body airway obstruction is achieved through a combination of back blows and chest thrusts. Abdominal thrusts are not recommended in infants and children because of their potential danger of injury to the abdominal organs, especially the liver.

If the victim is an infant, he is straddled over the rescuer's arm with the head lower than the trunk (Fig. 2). The head must be supported with a hand around the jaw and chest. For additional support, it is advisable for the rescuer to rest the forearm on his thigh. Four back blows are rapidly delivered with the heel of the hand between the infant's shoulder blades. Care must be exercised, since much less force needs to be exerted than in the adult. Immediately after delivering the back blows, the rescuer places his free hand on the infant's back so that the victim is sandwiched between the two hands, one supporting the neck, jaw, and chest, while the other is in a position to support the back. While continuing

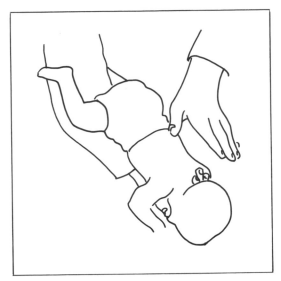

Figure 2.—Infant, back blows.

to provide support to the head and neck, the victim is turned and placed on the thigh with the head lower than the trunk, and four chest thrusts are delivered in rapid succession in the same manner as external chest compressions are performed in the infant (Fig. 1, lower panel).

If the victim is a child, too large to straddle the rescuer's forearm, the rescuer kneels on the floor and drapes the victim across the thighs, keeping the head lower than the trunk.

The four back blows can be delivered with somewhat greater force than that used for the infant. With the head and back supported, the child is rolled over onto the floor and is now in position for the four chest thrusts. These are applied in the same manner as external chest compression is applied for the child.

Blind finger sweeps are to be avoided in infants and children, since the foreign body can easily be pushed back and cause further obstruction. In the unconscious victim, immediately after the chest thrusts, the tongue and lower jaw are lifted forward and the mouth opened. This is done by placing the thumb in the victim's mouth over the tongue; the other fingers are wrapped around the lower jaw. If the foreign body is visualized, it may be removed with a finger.

If the victim has not started breathing after this maneuver, the airway should again be opened and a seal made over the mouth or the mouth-nose of the victim and an attempt made to deliver four breaths. If the chest does not rise, the obstruction persists, and its relief must again be sought via the aforementioned technique.

Circulation

Checking the Pulse—Once the airway has been opened and four breaths delivered, it must be determined whether only breathing has stopped or whether a cardiac arrest has also occurred. Cardiac arrest is recognized by absence of a pulse in the large arteries in an unconscious victim who is not breathing. The pulse in a child can be felt over the carotid artery in a manner similar to that described for the adult. The feeling of a pulse in an infant is more of a problem. Unfortunately, the very short and at times fat neck of an infant makes the carotid pulse difficult to feel. Precordial activity represents an impulse rather than a pulse and has been found not to be reliable. Some infants with good cardiac activity may have a quiet precordium, leading to the erroneous impression that chest compression is indicated. Because of this difficulty, it is recommended that in infants the brachial pulse be checked. With practice, this can be as easily mastered as palpatating a carotid pulse.

The brachial pulse is located on the inside of the upper arm, midway between the elbow and the shoulder (Fig. 3). The rescuer's thumb is placed on the outside of the arm, between the shoulder and the elbow. The tips of the index and middle fingers are placed on the opposite side of the arm. The index and middle fingers are pressed lightly toward the bone until the pulse is felt.

When there is a pulse but no breathing, then only breathing has arrested. Rescue breathing must continue as long as the infant or child cannot breathe for himself. Ventilation should be **gentle**—just enough to make the chest rise—and if the infant or child is struggling for breath, ventilation should be coordinated with the victim's respiratory effort. As the victim attempts to breathe **in**, the rescuer should breathe **out** into the victim's lungs.

Anyone observing an infant or child breathing will note that the smaller the child, the more rapid is the natural breathing rate. Breathing rates for infants and children under conditions of resuscitation should be more rapid than for adults according to the following rates: (1) Infant—breathe once every three seconds or 20 times per minute; (2) Child—breathe once every four seconds or 15 times per minute.

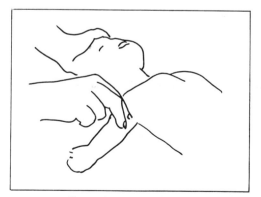

Figure 3.—Brachial pulse.

External Chest Compression — If the victim's pulse is not palpable, then a combination of rescue breathing and chest compression is indicated to circulate the blood around the body. Rescue breathing alone is indicated when breathing has stopped, but a pulse is still palpable. Chest compression is never performed without rescue breathing. It is in the technique of external chest compression that differences between infants, children, and adults become most apparent. The differences are related to the position of the heart within the chest, the small size of the chest, and the faster heart rate of the infant and child as compared with that of the adult.

Position of the Heart — As the chest grows, the proportion occupied by the heart diminishes. The heart in the infant and child is situated higher in the chest than it is in the adult. The proper area of compression in the **infant** is the midsternum (Fig. 1, lower panel). If an imaginary line is drawn between the nipples, the proper area of compression is the midportion of this line. A **child's** heart is lower than an infant's but not as low as an adult's. Using the technique as described for the adult, the notch in the center of the chest is located with the middle finger. The area just above the index finger is the appropriate area of compression in the **child.**

The chest of an infant or child is smaller and more pliable than that of an adult. Two hands are not necessary for proper compression. In an **infant**, two or three fingers are adequate (Fig. 1, lower panel). With the fingers on the midsternum (between nipples), the breastbone is compressed ½ to 1 inch (1.3 to 2.5 cm). The victim should lie on a hard surface for the rescuer to achieve best results. In the **child**, more force will have to be exerted. If the infant or child is large enough so that the sternum will not easily compress with three fingers, the heel of one hand will be needed. Only the heel of the hand should be used; the fingers must be kept off the chest. If the victim is large enough to require the heel of the hand for compression, the depth should be increased to 1 to 1½ inches (2.5 to 3.8 cm).

Because of the inherently faster heart rate in infants and children, the compression rate must also be faster as follows: (1) Infants — 100 compressions per minute; (2) Children — 80 compressions per minute.

External chest compression must always be accompanied by rescue breathing, and the two must be coordinated. The ratio of compressions to respirations is 5:1, both for single and for two rescuers. In infants and small children, backward tilt of the head lifts the back. A firm support beneath the back is therefore required for external chest compression and can be provided by the rescuer slipping one hand beneath the child's back while using the other hand to compress the chest. A folded blanket or other adjunct can also be used beneath the back to provide support. This helps to maintain head tilt and an open airway. Head tilt can also be maintained by utilizing the hand not performing compressions. When only a single rescuer is present, after each fifth compression a breath is interposed without stopping compressions. A brief pause is acceptable if necessary.

Compressions should be counted by the rescuer performing the compression as follows: (1) Infant — One, two, three, four, five, breathe; (2) Child — One and two and three and four and five and breathe.

—Excerpted from the Journal of the American Medical Association, "Standards and Guidelines for Cardiopulmonary Resuscitation and Emergency Cardiac Care," copyright 1979 by The American Heart Association. Used with permission.